Drones
WITHDRAWN

Jodie Mangor

Rourke
Educational Media

rourkeeducationalmedia.com

D1541813

Teaching Focus:
Concepts of Print- Have students find capital letters and punctuation in a sentence. Ask students to explain the purpose for using them in a sentence.

Before Reading:

Building Academic Vocabulary and Background Knowledge

Before reading a book, it is important to set the stage for your child or student by using pre-reading strategies. This will help them develop their vocabulary, increase their reading comprehension, and make connections across the curriculum.

1. *Read the title and look at the cover. Let's make predictions about what this book will be about.*
2. *Take a picture walk by talking about the pictures/photographs in the book. Implant the vocabulary as you take the picture walk. Be sure to talk about the text features such as headings, the Table of Contents, glossary, bolded words, captions, charts/diagrams, or index.*
3. *Have students read the first page of text with you then have students read the remaining text.*
4. *Strategy Talk – use to assist students while reading.*
   - *Get your mouth ready*
   - *Look at the picture*
   - *Think…does it make sense*
   - *Think…does it look right*
   - *Think…does it sound right*
   - *Chunk it – by looking for a part you know*
5. *Read it again.*
6. *After reading the book, complete the activities below.*

Content Area Vocabulary
Use glossary words in a sentence.

force
pilot
propeller
remote control
rotor
sensors

After Reading:

Comprehension and Extension Activity

After reading the book, work on the following questions with your child or students in order to check their level of reading comprehension and content mastery.

1. *What are some things drones may be used for in the future? (Summarize)*
2. *Name some things drones are used for. (Asking questions)*
3. *How do drones know what to do? (Text to self connection)*
4. *Explain how a quadcopter works. (Inferring)*

Extension Activity

With the help of an adult, browse the Internet and find out more facts about how drones are used and what the future of drones may be. Using a piece of construction paper and markers, design and draw your own drone. Label all its parts. Below the picture, list 10 things you would use your drone for that may help scientists learn more about the environment, further search and rescue missions, or whatever you can think of to put these amazing machines to good use!

Table of Contents

What is a Drone? 4

Breaking it Down......................................10

In the Air, On the Move! 16

Photo Glossary 22

Index 24

Websites To Visit 24

About the Author 24

What is a Drone?

What is that up in the sky?

It's a bird ... it's a **remote control** airplane ... no, it's a drone!

There may be 30,000 drones flying overhead in the United States by the year 2020.

Drones are a special kind of flying machine. They have no **pilot** on board. Instead, someone on the ground controls them.

Drones can go places and do things that are too dangerous for a regular airplane.

Drones come in many sizes and shapes.

Some drones are as small as an insect.

Some drones are military machines.

Others, like quadcopters, are used for both work and fun.

Breaking it Down

A quadcopter is a type of drone with four motors. Each motor turns a **rotor**, which spins a **propeller**.

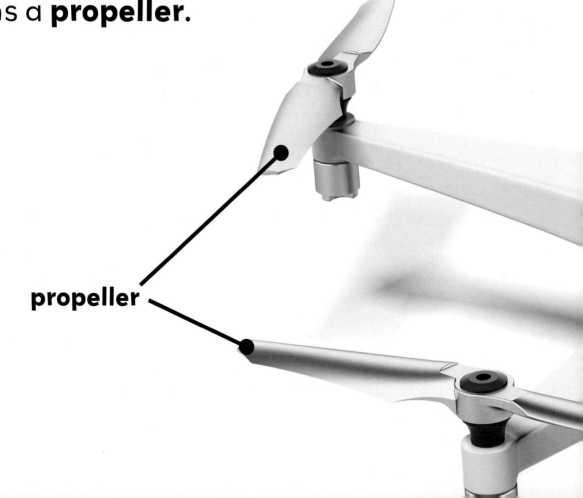

propeller

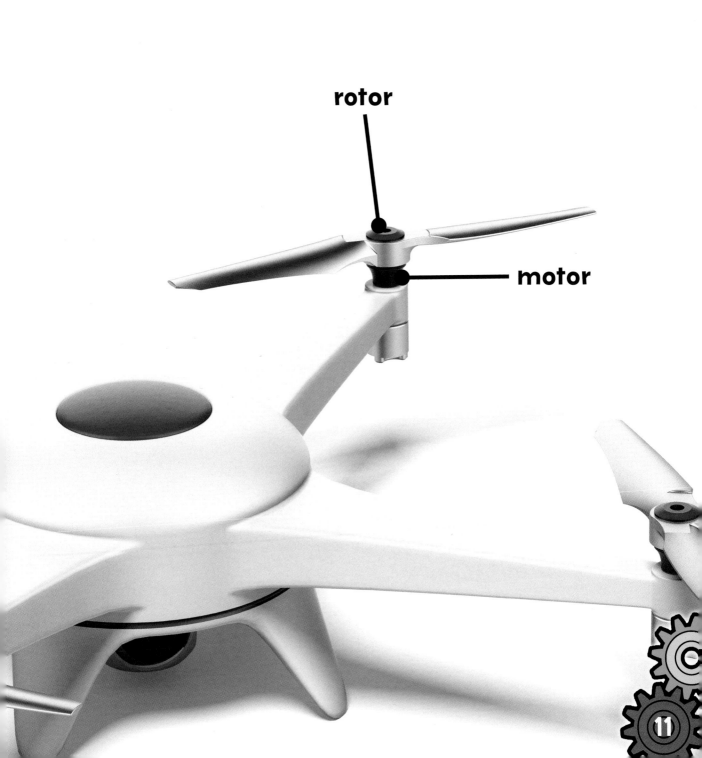

rotor

motor

The spinning propellers create a **force** called lift. This force allows the quadcopter to rise up into the air.

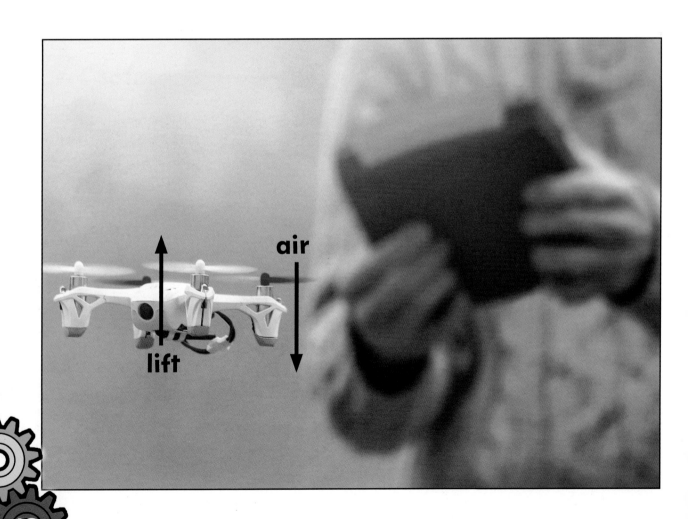

air

lift

Two rotors spin in one direction and two spin in the other. This helps with flight and balance.

Drones have **sensors** to help them stay level while flying. They can carry cameras or other equipment.

A battery supplies the drone with power. A strong, light frame holds all its parts together.

In the Air, On the Move!

How does a drone know what to do? The person flying it has a handheld unit called a controller. It communicates with a tiny computer inside the drone. The pilot uses it to tell the drone how to move.

Radio waves carry orders from the controller to the drone.

Drones have many uses. They help scientists collect information about plants, animals, and the weather.

They help businesses inspect pipelines and spray crops. They can be used for search and rescue missions.

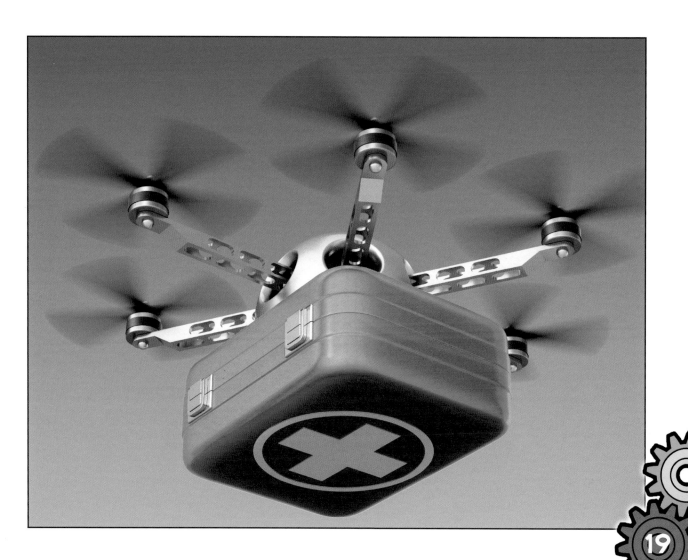

People keep thinking of new ways to use drones. Soon they may deliver goods to your door!

Flying drones can be a fun hobby. Almost anyone can own a drone.

Photo Glossary

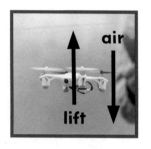

force (fors): Any action that produces, stops or changes the movement of an object.

pilot (PYE-luht): A person who flies an aircraft.

propeller (pruh-PEL-ur): A set of rotating blades that cause an object to move through air or water.

remote control (ri-MOHT kuhn-TROHL): A device for controlling something from a distance.

rotor (ROH-tur): A part of a machine that turns around a central point.

sensors (SEN-surz): Instruments that can detect changes and send the information to a controlling device.

Index

battery 15

controller 16, 17

military 9

motor(s) 10, 11

pilot 6, 16

propeller(s) 10, 12

quadcopter(s) 9, 10, 12

uses 16, 18

Websites to Visit

www.khanacademy.org/partner-content/mit-k12/mit-k12-physics/v/
    indoor-flying-robots

thekidshouldseethis.com/post/16922370178

mocomi.com/drones

About the Author

Jodie Mangor writes magazine articles, books, and audio scripts for children. While writing this book, she and her 9-year-old son learned how to fly a mini-quadcopter. Jodie lives in Ithaca, New York, with her family.

Meet The Author!
www.meetREMauthors.com

© 2017 Rourke Educational Media

www.rourkeeducationalmedia.com

PHOTO CREDITS: Cover ©egw3D; title page ©Alex Salcedo; p.4-5 © Chrisboswell; p.6 ©p_ponomareva; p.7 ©John Cater; p.8 © Serbi; p.9 © everlite; p.10-11, 22, 23 ©ekostsov; p.12, 22 ©Gregory Dubus; p.13 ©Voyagerix; p.14 ©Maxiphoto; p.15, 23 ©Marek Vliasz; p. 17 ©Ivan Nezdoiminoga; p. 17, 22, 23 ©Thatsaphon Saengnarongrat; p.18 © valio84sl; p.19, 20 ©mipan; p.21 ©Vladimir Vitek

Edited by: Keli Sipperley
Designed by: Jen Thomas

Library of Congress PCN Data

Drones / Jodie Mangor
(How It Works)
ISBN 978-1-68191-686-6 (hard cover)(alk. paper)
ISBN 978-1-68191-787-0 (soft cover)
ISBN 978-1-68191-886-0 (e-Book)
Library of Congress Control Number: 2016932562

Printed in the United States of America, North Mankato, Minnesota

Also Available as:

ROURKE'S
e-Books